Microwave Man

Percy Spencer and His Sizzling Invention

Sara L. Latta

Enslow Elementary
an imprint of
Enslow Publishers, Inc.
40 Industrial Road
Box 398
Berkeley Heights, NJ 07922
USA

http://www.enslow.com

Enslow Elementary, an imprint of Enslow Publishers, Inc.

Enslow Elementary® is a registered trademark of Enslow Publishers, Inc.

Library of Congress Cataloging-in-Publication Data

Latta, Sara L.
  Microwave man : Percy Spencer and his sizzling invention / by Sara L. Latta.
      p. cm. — (Inventors at work!)
  Summary: "Read about Percy's early life, his work with radar tubes, and find out how he invented the mircrowave"—Provided by publisher.
  Includes bibliographical references and index.
  ISBN 978-0-7660-4201-8
  1. Spencer, Percy, 1894-1970—Juvenile literature. 2. Raytheon Company—Employees—Biography—Juvenile literature. 3. Electrical engineers—United States—Biography—Juvenile literature. 4. Inventors—Biography—Juvenile literature. 5. Microwave ovens—Juvenile literature. I. Title. II. Title: Percy Spencer and his sizzling invention.
  TK140.S64L38 2014
  609.2—dc23
                              2012041457

Future editions:
Paperback ISBN: 978-1-4644-0345-3
EPUB ISBN: 978-1-4645-1191-2
Single-User PDF ISBN: 978-1-4646-1191-9
Multi-User PDF ISBN: 978-0-7660-5823-1

Printed in the United States of America
102013 Lake Book Manufacturing, Inc., Melrose Park, IL
10 9 8 7 6 5 4 3 2 1

Photo Credits: Gwen Shockey/Science Source, Inc., p. 16; Image NRL1907, courtesy of the Naval History & Heritage Command, p. 11; KirtBlattenberger/RF Café, p. 18; Photos.com, p. 8; Public domain image, p. 33; Shutterstock.com, pp. 1, 4, 14, 39, 40, 41, 42, 43; SeanPavonePhoto/Photos.com, p. 34; © Spencer Family Archives, pp. 1, 6, 12, 20, 21, 23, 25, 26, 28, 31, 37.

Cover Photo: Photo of Percy Spencer: © Spencer Family Archives; Clipart: Shutterstock.com

CONTENTS

A Boy Who Loved to Learn

Pop, pop, pop! Mmmm . . . popcorn, warm and buttery. Making popcorn, heating a cup of cocoa, or cooking frozen pizza is fast and easy with a microwave oven. Nine out of ten kitchens in the United States have one of these time-saving devices. The next time you use a microwave oven, think of its inventor, Percy Spencer.

In 1945, no one had thought of using microwaves to cook or heat food. Not even Percy himself! But one day, the scientist became curious about a melted candy bar in his pocket. The microwave oven is the result of his curiosity.

Percy Spencer and his brother, Al, were born in this house in Maine.

Percy was born in the summer of 1894, in the small town of Howland, Maine. When he was just a tot, his father died in an accident at work. Percy's mother was so sad that she could not take care of him or his older brother, Al. She left Percy in the care of a couple that he called his aunt and uncle. They cared for him and loved him as if he were their own son. Al went to live with another family nearby.

A Boyhood in Maine

Percy and his Uncle Henry liked to fix things. Percy spent many hours exploring the broken machines that his uncle brought home to fix. Percy also loved nature and animals. He spent much of his free time in the woods.

Then, when Percy was seven years old, a terrible thing happened. His dear uncle died. Percy and his aunt grew very poor. Percy quit school before he finished fifth grade so that he could help his aunt make money.

Brave radio operators aboard the sinking *Titanic* inspired Percy Spencer to become a radio operator himself.

Some boys might have felt sorry for themselves. Not Percy. Every dawn, he walked to his job at a spool mill. He worked until the sun set. He read books and studied on his own. He taught himself everything he could about machines.

When Percy was sixteen years old, he learned that a nearby paper mill wanted to switch from using steam power to electric power. Few people knew much about using electric power in 1910. Percy didn't know much about electric power either. He was curious and eager to learn. He signed up to work with two other men. By the time they finished bringing electric power to the paper mill, Percy was an expert.

On to the Navy

When the *Titanic* steamed out of the harbor in 1912, it carried a new invention: the wireless telegraph. The wireless telegraph used radio waves to send and receive coded messages.

Several days into the voyage, the mighty ship hit an iceberg and began to sink. Radio operators on board sent out calls for help. A nearby ship heard the call. It changed course to rescue the survivors.

Eighteen-year-old Percy read about the brave radio operators on the *Titanic*. He wanted to be a radio operator, too. He joined the Navy and entered its radio school. He knew that he had a lot to learn. "I just got hold of a lot of textbooks and taught myself while I was standing watch at night," he said.

World War I began while Percy was in the Navy. Now, his talent for working with radio sets and other machines became even more important.

Percy Spencer was in the Navy until 1915. This class is part of the Naval Radio School in Cambridge, Massachusetts.

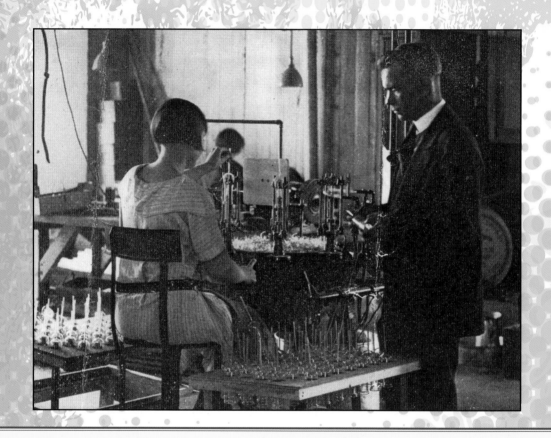

This photo shows Percy Spencer working at Raytheon during his first year at the company, 1925.

Making a Name for Himself

Percy Spencer left the Navy in 1915. He went to work for a company in Boston that made radios. As always, he wanted to learn how things worked. He read and read. He often worked late into the night to get his job done. Soon, he was in charge of a team that made radios. Everyone knew that they could count on Spencer. He continued to work with the Navy to help radio operators who had problems.

Spencer found himself wanting to learn more about how people could use electricity. In 1925, he joined the company where his brother, Al, worked. The men who started the company wanted to use radio waves to make housework easier. The company soon changed its name to Raytheon.

What Are Waves?

Have you ever thrown a rock into a pond? A small pebble will create small ripples in the water. Each wave is close to the next one. They have short wavelengths. If you throw a bigger rock into the lake, you will create bigger waves. They are spaced farther apart. They have long wavelengths.

The energy from the sun and other objects in outer space also travels to Earth in waves. We call them electromagnetic waves. Some have wavelengths shorter than an atom. Others can be longer than a football field. Together, all of these waves are called the electromagnetic spectrum.

When you listen to the radio or watch TV, you are using radio waves. They are good at carrying information from one place to another. When you talk on a cell phone, you are using microwaves.

ELECTROMAGNETIC SPECTRUM

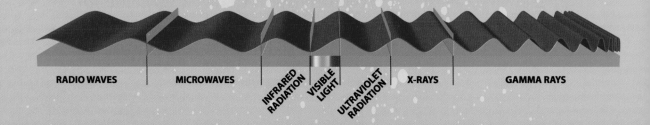

RADIO WAVES   MICROWAVES   INFRARED RADIATION   VISIBLE LIGHT   ULTRAVIOLET RADIATION   X-RAYS   GAMMA RAYS

Tiny Tubes and the War

Percy Spencer made a name for himself at Raytheon. He became an expert at creating a special kind of tube. The tube was important for sending and receiving radio signals. One scientist said, "Spencer . . . could make a working tube out of a sardine can."

Spencer was always looking for ways to make things work better. One time, he wanted to find a way to put some radio controls in his sons' model airplanes. Regular tubes would be too big. So he made tiny tubes that the toy airplanes could carry.

People at Raytheon saw the tiny tubes and knew they could be useful. In fact, they became very important in making better weapons during World War II.

In 1940, Great Britain was at war with Germany. Enemy planes dropped bomb after bomb on England. British pilots had a secret, though. They had found a way to use radar to learn of approaching enemy planes.

RADAR

Have you ever heard your echo? Echoes are sound waves that bounce off objects and return to you. By measuring the time it takes your echo to arrive, you can figure out the distance to the object. Radar works much the same way. It uses very short radio waves, or microwaves, instead of sound waves. Radar is short for "*RAdio Detection And Ranging.*"

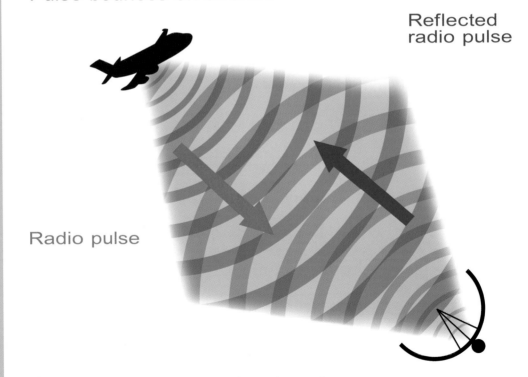

Pulse bounces off aircraft

Reflected radio pulse

Radio pulse

Rotating radio transmitter/receiver

But there was a problem. They could not make the radar sets fast enough. At the heart of the radar set was a tube. The tube changed electric power to microwaves. It took a week just to make one radar tube. They needed thousands of radar tubes and they needed them fast!

Spencer to the Rescue

British scientists asked Raytheon and other American companies for help. One Friday, Spencer met with one of the scientists. He studied the radar tube closely. "I wonder if I could take this home over the weekend?" he asked.

real fact!

The name *Raytheon* means a beam of light (ray) from the gods (*theon*, a Greek word).

Because of Percy Spencer's smart thinking, a World War II radar tube could be manufactured 600 times faster than before.

It was one of Great Britain's top military secrets! The British scientist trusted Spencer. He let him take it home.

On Monday, Spencer returned to work with a smile on his face. He had figured out a way to make many radar tubes quickly. Using Spencer's method, production of the radar tube jumped from seventeen per week to 2,600 per day.

Military experts say that the radar tube was a key factor in winning World War II.

Brother Al

When Al Spencer was fifteen, he had a job at a mill in Maine. He kept the furnace filled with burning wood to power the mill's steam engine.

Al noticed something interesting. When the furnace was very hot, the door in the top of the boiler would pop out in a shallow dome. When the furnace cooled down, the door popped down to its usual flat shape. He

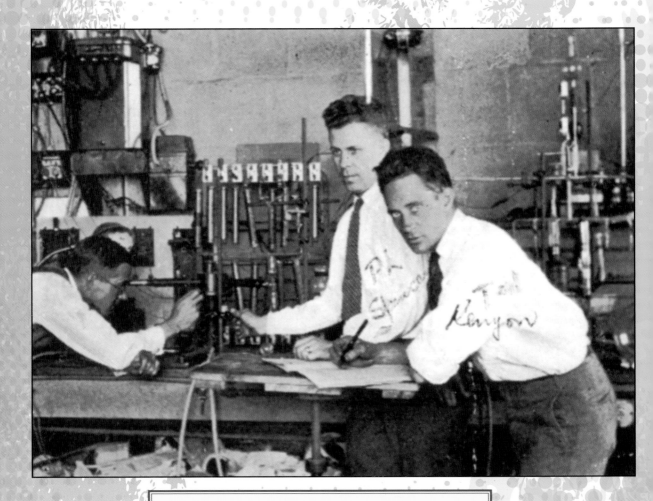

Percy Spencer (center) working at Raytheon in 1925

realized that the door was telling him when it was time to add more fuel to the furnace. All he had to do was listen for the second pop.

When Al was working at Raytheon, he remembered that door. He made a metal disc that would snap out at a certain temperature. Spencer Discs are still used today to control temperatures in everything from coffee makers to ovens.

The Spencer Disc

3

The Melting Candy Bar

Raytheon had a problem. They had become very good at making radar tubes. But the war was coming to an end. The military no longer needed thousands of radar tubes. Raytheon needed to make something that ordinary people could use.

Percy Spencer's boss kept a copy of the book *The Little Engine That Could* in his office. "I think I can, I think I can" was his motto. He wanted his scientists to believe that they could solve any problem. He asked them, "What shall we do after the war?"

Percy Spencer had a long career working at Raytheon. And because of a candy bar melting in his pocket, he eventually invented the microwave oven.

All of the scientists at Raytheon knew that the radar tubes could make some things heat up. In the winter, they often warmed their cold hands by the warmth of the radar tubes. How could they use this knowledge?

Now He's Cookin'

Spencer often carried a peanut candy bar in his pocket so that he could feed birds and squirrels whenever he got the chance. One day, when Spencer was walking through one of the company's labs, he stopped in front of a radar tube. He noticed something strange. His candy bar was melting!

Spencer had been thinking hard about how they could use microwave heating. He wondered whether microwaves could be used to cook food.

Spencer asked someone to bring him a bag of unpopped popcorn. He placed the bag in front of the radar tube and turned it on. Sure enough, the kernels quickly popped!

Percy Spencer (right) and the other scientists at Raytheon knew that radar tubes could heat things up.

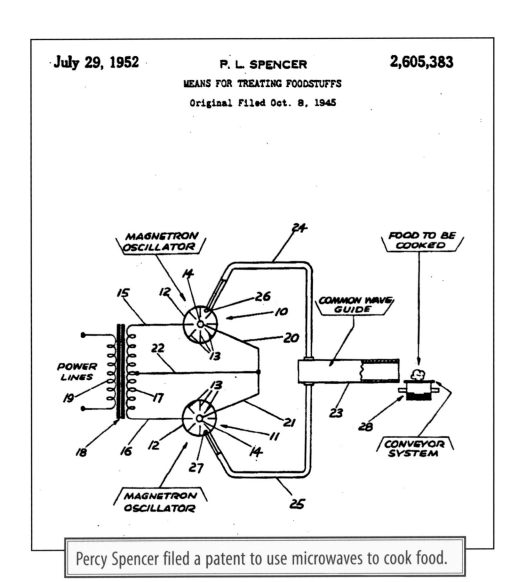

Percy Spencer filed a patent to use microwaves to cook food.

The next day, Spencer brought to work a raw egg in its shell. He put the egg in front of the radar tube. At first, nothing happened. A curious co-worker leaned in closer. Suddenly, the egg exploded. The man had cooked egg all over his face. It was a mess!

Spencer knew they were on to something. In October 1945, he filed for a patent to use microwaves to cook food. With the help of another man at Raytheon, he built a simple oven with two radar tubes inside.

They had a contest to name their new oven. Since the oven had its roots in radar systems, the winner was "Radar range." Those words were later combined to Radarange®. This was the name of the first microwave oven.

How Do Microwaves Cook Food?

When microwaves move through food, they make molecules of water, sugar, and some fats shake and spin. In fact, water molecules can spin millions of times a second when they are hit by microwaves. All of this spinning and shaking creates heat, which cooks the food.

Radarange Unit Model 1161A

The Radarange® was the first microwave oven. Look how big it was!

Microwaves can go straight through most kinds of paper, plastic, or glass. Many of these materials are safe to use in the microwave. But microwaves cannot go through metal. When microwaves hit the metal, they bounce right off and can harm certain parts of the microwave oven. This is why you should never put anything made of metal in a microwave oven. You should also never run an empty microwave oven. If there is no food to take in the microwaves, they can damage the microwave.

The First Microwave Ovens

The first microwave oven was sold to a restaurant in Cleveland, Ohio, in 1947. It cost $3,000. The monster weighed 750 pounds and stood five and a half feet tall. It had a water pipe to cool the oven's radio tube and used a lot of power. This was no oven for a home kitchen!

That year, the American public got a chance to use a microwave oven in a New York City train station. The "Speedy Weeny" was a microwave oven inside a vending machine. People loved the idea of getting a quick hot dog from a machine!

The first microwave oven was sold to a restaurant in Ohio.

For twenty years, the Radarange® was sold mostly to restaurants, railroads, and ocean liners. Cooks liked the fact that they could keep their food fresh in the refrigerator until a customer ordered something. Then, it took just a few minutes to heat up the order.

Microwaves in the Home

It was not until 1967 that Raytheon was able to make a microwave oven small and cheap enough for use in home kitchens. The Radarange® sold for $495. It took several years for it to become popular. But by 1975, there were more microwave ovens sold than gas stoves.

One of the problems with the first microwave ovens is that they leaked microwave energy. People worried that the leaked energy could cause burns or other health problems. Microwave oven makers changed their design so that they no longer leaked. Some people worried about microwave radiation. They

Announcing the most important advancement in microwave ovens in years...

Amana *Radarange*
MICROWAVE OVEN
ROTAWAVE™ Cooking System

Model RR-10A

A rotating shower of power that cooks more evenly...and cooks most foods faster than ever before.

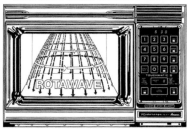

Another Amana first . . . the exclusive Amana Rotawave Cooking System employs a completely new technology that cooks so evenly most foods require no turning and cook even faster than before.

Here's why. *The Amana Rotawave system uses a rotating antenna* which beams microwave energy directly at food in a uniform, rotating pattern. The results are remarkable:

Foods cook more evenly, more conveniently
Virtually all foods . . . large or small . . . cook more uniformly throughout. Even multiple items like rows of cookies bake more evenly than ever before. And most foods require no turning because the Rotawave antenna constantly rotates the microwaves through the food.

Features that make the Amana Touchmatic II™ the most advanced Radarange ever made.
- Cooks by time.
- Cooks to selected temperature.
- Holds food at temperature to tenderize economy cuts of meat.
- Defrosts and cooks by memory.
- Automatic Start Time—starts cooking while you're away.
- Wide range of Cookmatic™ cooking speeds.
- Stainless steel interior. Cleanup is a snap.
- So automatic, it even remembers the time of day.

No wonder Amana Radarange Microwave Ovens are the first choice of so many people. For further information see your Amana Retailer or write Ann MacGregor, Department 741, Amana, Iowa 52204.

This famous Amana cap is worn by many of the Tours' leading players. Watch for them on the leader board.

If it doesn't say *Amana*-it's not a *Radarange*
MICROWAVE OVEN

BACKED BY A CENTURY-OLD TRADITION OF FINE CRAFTSMANSHIP.

Amana Refrigeration, Inc., Amana, Iowa 52204   A Raytheon Company

217

This is an advertisement for the Radarange®.

Safety tips for cooking in a microwave oven:

- Ask an adult to help if you are using a microwave oven for the first time.

- Use cookware that is specially made for use in the microwave.

- Many microwave ovens have special buttons for different food items. If you are not sure how long to cook something, it is best to cook your food for thirty seconds at a time. Carefully check your food. If it is not quite done, heat for another thirty seconds.

- Use a potholder when removing a dish from the microwave. Open any lids away from your face so that the steam does not burn you.

- Stir your food before tasting. Food sometimes heats unevenly in microwave ovens.

- If you are making a frozen meal or popcorn, follow the instructions on the package.

were afraid that food cooked with microwaves would cause cancer or other diseases.

Some forms of very high-energy electromagnetic waves, like X-rays and gamma rays, can cause cancer. But microwaves, like the light you can see, have much lower energies. They do not make food dangerous to eat.

A College Degree

Percy Spencer had helped make Raytheon a powerful company. By 1950, he had 138 patents. Many, like the ones for using microwaves to cook food, changed our lives. But he did not always get the respect he deserved. Most other scientists had gone to college. They studied even more after graduating from college to get another degree. Spencer had not even finished fifth grade.

The University of Massachusetts decided that he deserved better. They gave him an honorary degree. It was a great moment for Spencer. He was proud to be called Dr. Percy Spencer. One of his co-workers at Raytheon said, "He has earned it far more than most [people] I know."

Percy Spencer was proud to be called Dr. Spencer.

That same year, Spencer became vice president of Raytheon. He kept working at making his tubes better and better. He liked to get to work by 7 A.M. so that he could talk to the people working the night shift. "I let my people know I care," he said. "When you work nights you think nobody cares what you do. I know; I used to be there."

Percy Spencer was an orphan who never finished grammar school. But he had a great desire to learn. He said that he decided to solve "his own situation." Because of his wartime accomplishments, the U.S. Navy gave Spencer a medal. He died in 1970 at the age of 76.

In just a few years, the microwave oven would become one of the most common kitchen devices. Percy Spencer entered the Inventors Hall of Fame in 1999.

Thanks to Percy Spencer, people are able to enjoy hot food quickly and easily.

So you want to be an inventor? You can do it! First, you need a terrific idea.

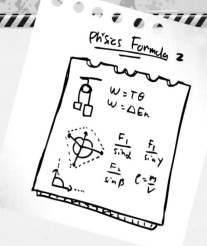

Got a Problem? No Problem!

Many inventions begin when someone thinks of a great solution to a problem. One cold day in 1994, ten-year-old K.K. Gregory was building a snow fort. Soon, she had snow between her mittens and her coat sleeve. Her wrists were cold and wet. She found some scraps of fabric around the house and used them to make a tube that would fit around her wrist. She cut a thumb hole in the tube to make a kind of fingerless glove and called it a "Wristie." Wearing mittens over her new invention, her wrists stayed nice and warm when she played outside. Today, the Wristie business is booming.

Now it's your turn. Maybe, like K.K. Gregory, you have an idea for something new that would make your life better or easier. Perhaps you can think of a way to improve an everyday item. Twelve-year-old Becky Schroeder became one of the youngest people ever to receive a U.S. patent after she invented a glow-in-the-dark clipboard that allowed people to write in the dark. Do you like to play sports or board games? James Naismith, inspired by a game he used to play as a boy, invented a new game he called basketball.

Let your imagination run wild. You never know where it will take you.

Research It!

Okay, you have a terrific idea for an invention. Now what do you do?

First, you will want to make sure that nobody else has thought of your idea.

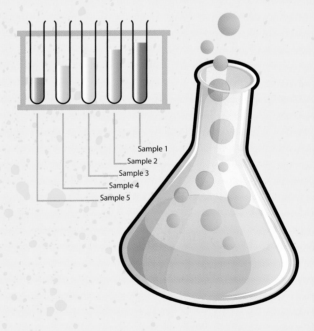

Sample 1
Sample 2
Sample 3
Sample 4
Sample 5

You wouldn't want to spend hours developing your new invention, only to find that someone else beat you to it. Check out Google Patents (see Learn More for the Web site address), which can help you find out whether your idea is original.

Bring It to Life!

If no one else has thought of your idea, congratulations! Write it down in a notebook. Date and initial every entry you make. If you file a patent for your invention later, this will help you prove that you were the first to think of it. The most important thing about this logbook is that pages cannot be added or subtracted. You can buy a bound notebook at any office supply store.

Draw several different pictures of your invention in your logbook. Try sketching views from above, below, and to the side. Show how big each part of your invention should be.

Build a model. Don't be discouraged if it doesn't work at first. You may have to experiment with different designs and materials. That's part of the fun! Take pictures of everything, and tape them into your logbook. Try your invention out on your friends and family. If they have any suggestions to make it better, build another model. Perfect your invention, and give it a clever name.

Patent It!

Do you want to sell your invention? You'll want to apply for a patent. Holding a patent to your invention means that no one else can make, use, or sell your invention in the United States without your  permission. It prevents others from making money off your idea. You will definitely need an adult to help you apply for a patent. It can be a complicated and expensive process. But if you think that people will want to buy your invention, it is well worth it. Good luck!

1894 Percy Spencer is born in Howland, Maine, on July 19.

1896 Spencer's father dies. His mother leaves him with a kindly couple who Spencer calls aunt and uncle.

1901 Spencer's uncle dies.

1906 Spencer goes to work at a spool mill.

1910 Spencer gets a job at a paper mill to help install an electrical system.

1912 The *Titanic* sinks; Spencer joins the Navy to learn wireless telegraphy.

1914 World War I begins.

1915 Spencer leaves the Navy and takes a job with the Wireless Specialty Apparatus Company in Boston.

1918 World War I ends.

1921 Spencer marries Louise Larsen, of Worcester, Massachusetts.

1925 Raytheon hires Spencer.

1939 World War II begins.

1941 Spencer finds a way to make many radio tubes at once for British radar.

1945 World War II ends.

1945 Spencer's candy bar melts. He gets the idea for using microwaves to cook food.

1947 The first microwave oven is sold.

1967 The first countertop microwave made specifically for household kitchens is introduced.

1970 Spencer dies on September 8. He is 76 years old.

1999 Spencer enters Inventors Hall of Fame. He received over 300 patents during his career.

electromagnetic waves—Waves of energy with electric and magnetic fields.

gamma rays—Electromagnetic waves with very short wavelengths.

microwave—A type of short radio wave.

molecule—A group of atoms bonded together.

patent—An official paper that gives an inventor the only right to make, use, or sell an invention for a certain number of years.

radio wave—An electromagnetic wave with a very long wavelength.

wireless—An early form of radio.

LEARN MORE

Books

Bridgman, Roger. *1000 Inventions and Discoveries.* New York: DK Children, 2006.

Platt, Richard. *Eureka! Great Inventions and How They Happened.* Boston: Kingfisher, 2003.

St. George, Judith. *So You Want to Be an Inventor?* New York: Puffin Books, 2005.

Taylor, Barbara. *I Wonder Why Zippers Have Teeth: And Other Questions About Inventions.* Boston: Kingfisher, 2003.

Web Sites

Google Patents. <http://google.com/patents>

KidsGeo.com. "Microwave Sensing." <http://www.kidsgeo.com/geography-for-kids/0038-microwave-and-radar-sensing.php>

The National Aeronautics and Space Administration. "The Electromagnetic Spectrum." <http://science.hq.nasa.gov/kids/imagers/ems/index.html>

INDEX